LOVE PREVAILS

by

Tonya Renee Smith

ISBN: 978-1-960853-71-4

Liberation's Publishing House – Columbus, MS

-God Provides.

Table of Contents

1 DECISIONS, DECISIONS, DECISIONS

The time had arrived for me to make a life-changing decision—one that would not only affect my life but my children's as well. I had been married for a few years, long enough to understand that prayer was a vital key in any marriage. But despite my faith, I felt completely lost. Everything in my life was falling apart. I began to sink into a deep depression, and once again, I considered suicide. I didn't want to go on.

I didn't know how to live without my security—Marvin. I asked God if I was making the right decision by divorcing my husband, especially after only a few short years of marriage. Was I supposed to overlook the cheating? Should I forgive and forget to honor the vows I had spoken before God and our families? The thought pierced my soul like a two-edged sword.

I had always pictured raising my children in a two-parent household. I never planned on being a single mother, raising two kids alone at such a young age. At this particular time, I was only in my late twenties, and for the sake of my family, I felt it was crucial to do everything in my power to keep the household together. A home with a stable mother and father. A home that was far from perfect but filled with love and tenderness.

See, I didn't grow up in a home with two parents. My mother had raised nine children on her own. Because of that, I was determined not to repeat the same cycle. I wanted to build a better marriage, one that could work—if only I could influence my straying husband to focus on what we shared: our children.

But deep down, I knew that Marvin's love for his once-beautiful, slender wife was changing. He didn't love me the way I was accustomed to, but I hoped he would soon realize that the kids needed their father in the home. They needed to see that when times get rough, love doesn't have to crumble. That two people facing difficulties can still find a way to make things work.

I was willing to try if he was.

I prayed every day that my broken marriage would be restored and renewed. I refused to give up on my family. I also couldn't ignore how the typical Black family was already stereotyped as broken and dysfunctional. That thought alone pushed me to fight even harder.

Encouraged by my friends, pastor, and other spiritual leaders, I agreed to consider couples counseling. It seemed like a good idea—after all, it couldn't hurt. We never truly talked to each other anymore, only at each other. Counseling could give us the opportunity to open up, to take responsibility for the parts we played in our failing marriage.

At one of my sessions, the counselor asked me to write down all of Marvin's great qualities on one side of the paper and his flaws on the other. Lo and behold, the flaws far outweighed the good. I was sure his list of my shortcomings looked the same.

It would take a miracle to fix this unfulfilling marriage.

Our relationship had been built on insecurities, not love. We were too young and naïve to understand what a genuine marriage required—hard work, dedication, prayer, and, most importantly, God's word.

But with God, nothing was impossible.

If this marriage was going to stand a fighting chance, we needed to be fully committed—not just as a couple, but as individuals. We had to make a crucial decision about our future, not just as partners, but as parents and human beings.

Prayerfully, love would prevail.

2 LITTLE GIRL LOST

I was at my wit's end with Marvin. I had endured too much heartache and pain to stay in this stressful, so-called "holy" matrimony any longer. I had tried all the techniques I was advised to practice, but nothing changed. We both knew our marriage was coming to an abrupt end. In a last-ditch effort to save our seven-year union, Marvin came up with a suggestion—he wanted to take me and the kids on a vacation.

It was an offer I couldn't refuse. We hadn't gone anywhere out of town since we got married, and I was sure the children would love the opportunity to have some fun. Maybe this trip was exactly what we needed—to mend our broken marriage, to relieve my mind of all the distress and trauma of a failing relationship.

Our marriage had been far from perfect, but I could see that Marvin was truly trying to keep our family together. So, we left our hometown of Vardaman, Mississippi, and set off for Memphis, Tennessee. Our destination? Libertyland®, an amusement park that would hopefully bring us some joy, even if just for the kids' sake.

We planned a two-day stay and were determined to enjoy every moment—leaving our worries and troubles behind, at least for now. I hadn't had any real fun, any "let your hair down" moments, since the day we said, "I do." This weekend was much needed.

Once we arrived and settled into our hotel, I had to admit—it was stunning. A luxury suite with a complimentary breakfast, an exercise room, a swimming pool, Wi-Fi, a full kitchen, and a beautiful balcony overlooking Memphis. The kids were thrilled to connect their game system to the TV, and for the first time in a long time, we all seemed to be at peace.

The Amusement Park Adventure

After quickly showering and dressing lightly—since the July heat was unbearable—we headed for Libertyland®. The amusement park was packed with tourists, just as eager as we were to enjoy the day. But as soon as we entered, a feeling of unease settled over me.

Something felt off.

Marvin spotted a rollercoaster and was eager to try it out. I, however, was hesitant. The park was massive and overflowing with people, and all I could think about were the horror stories I'd seen on the news—children being kidnapped or wandering off, never to be found again. I was not willing to take that risk just to ride a rollercoaster with my husband.

But Marvin insisted. He wanted us to enjoy ourselves for once. He wanted me to stop focusing on all the wrong in our marriage and try to embrace something positive. In his own way, he was desperately trying to heal the brokenness between us.

I still didn't trust him, but I agreed—on one condition: the kids had to be monitored closely. Marvin reassured me that his younger brother, John, who had come along on the trip, would watch over them.

I had no choice but to let my guard down and trust his judgment.

As we stood in line for the ride, I could feel my hands trembling. Marvin reached out, held my shaky, sweaty hand, and for a brief moment, it felt… nice. I had been so angry at him for his infidelities, so distant from him for so long. But at that moment, I allowed myself to feel comforted by his presence.

The rollercoaster ride ended, and to my surprise, I actually enjoyed it. I wasn't scared at all. But as we exited the ride, my heart sank into my stomach.

The kids were nowhere to be found.

A Parent's Worst Nightmare

I searched frantically, scanning the crowded park, but I couldn't see them. Panic set in. I turned to Marvin, screaming, "Where are the kids?!" My youngest, Alyssa—our six-year-old daughter—was missing. I lost all sense of logic. My heart pounded as fear suffocated me. This couldn't be happening.

Marvin's brother, John, had left her alone. He was just a teenager himself, eager to have fun, and instead of staying with Alyssa, he told her to wait in one spot while he went off to enjoy himself.

I was furious.

I had to calm down long enough to find a security officer. My body trembled, my breaths came in sharp gasps, and my chest ached so badly I thought I might need to be rushed to the hospital. But I had to push through—I had to find my daughter.

Minutes felt like hours as we searched.

I prayed.

I begged God not to let this nightmare be real.

Then, just as I was about to break completely, I looked up—and there she was. A security officer was walking toward me, holding my daughter's hand. I collapsed in relief, sobbing.

"You have a brave little girl," the officer said. "She came up to me and told me she was lost."

I was overcome with emotion—anger at Marvin, but pride for my daughter. She had been taught well, and she had handled herself wisely.

A Failed Attempt at Redemption

This vacation was supposed to save our marriage. Instead, it turned into a catastrophe. How did I convince myself that this sweet gesture could fix something so broken? I nearly had a heart attack. I almost ended up in the hospital. And worst of all, I almost lost my child. This was not the fresh start I had hoped for. This trip solidified what I had already known deep down—there was no saving this marriage. I couldn't do this anymore.

Once we returned home, I planned to move forward with the

divorce. Too much had happened. Too much had been broken. And for Marvin, I could only hope that somehow…

Love would prevail.

3 THE UNEXPECTED SURGERY

It was time for my annual check-up with my gynecologist, and deep down, I had a terrible feeling that something was wrong with my body. Stress had taken a toll on my mind, my health, and my overall well-being.

I had been losing weight rapidly, and the scary part? I wasn't even trying. I ate whatever I wanted—no dieting, no counting calories, no monitoring my sugar intake—yet the weight was falling off me at an alarming rate. My doctor was puzzled. He could tell something was wrong.

But I hadn't told him everything.

For the past year, I had been experiencing extremely heavy menstrual periods, but I never mentioned it during my previous appointments. In my family, this was common, and I didn't think there was anything a doctor could do about it. I figured I just needed to buy better feminine products and deal with it.

Then one day, while I was at work—standing, as usual, performing my duties as an inspector—I suddenly felt weak. I had no warning. No idea what was about to happen.

I passed out right there at my workstation.

A Terrifying Moment

When I regained consciousness, I was lying on the floor, surrounded by my co-workers. I could see the worry in their faces. Someone had already called an ambulance.

I had no memory of what had happened. I only knew one thing—something was terribly wrong.

At the hospital, after several tests, the nurse gave me shocking news: I had a fibroid tumor. It was the cause of my heavy bleeding. The reason I passed out at work. The nurse told me I needed to follow up with my gynecologist immediately. The urgency in her voice shook me. As soon as I left the hospital, I made the call. When they told me they could squeeze me in as a walk-in, I knew this was far more serious than I had imagined.

A Devastating Diagnosis

My husband was at work, so my mother and brother drove me to my doctor's appointment. As I stepped out of the car, I felt something warm running down my legs.

Blood.

It was gushing down uncontrollably.

Thank God I had worn black pants.

Horrified, I hurried into the clinic. I barely made it to the receptionist's desk before whispering, "Can I please go to the back waiting room?"

She glanced down and saw the blood pooling around my shoes. Her eyes widened in alarm. Without hesitation, she led me to a private area, and I rushed into the restroom to clean myself up. My hands trembled as I wiped away the blood, trying to compose myself, but I was completely distraught.

"How is this happening to me?" I thought.

I was only 29 years old.

A Life-Altering Decision

Dr. Whittle entered the examination room after reviewing my tests. His face was serious. My stomach twisted into knots.

"You need an emergency hysterectomy," he said.

The words hit me like a brick wall.

A hysterectomy?

I was not prepared for this.

Yes, I had two beautiful children, and I loved them more than life itself. But this surgery meant that any chance of having more children was gone forever.

I immediately thought about Marvin. Even though our marriage was already over, I knew deep down he had always wanted a son. How was I supposed to call him at work and tell him this?

Still, I had no choice.

I informed my mother and brother first. Then, I dialed Marvin's number. When I told him the news, he didn't hesitate. He left work and rushed to the hospital. By the time he arrived, I was being wheeled to my hospital room, where they would begin preparing me for surgery. I didn't know how to feel.

I had walked into that hospital as a woman, and now I knew I would be leaving without a part of what made me one.

A Cold, Heartbreaking Goodbye

There were so many myths about women who had hysterectomies.

"You won't be able to satisfy a man anymore."

"You'll lose your passion."

"Your marriage will never survive it."

So many ugly thoughts raced through my mind.

As the nurse prepared to wheel me to the operating room, Marvin and his friend walked in. The nurse smiled warmly at them and asked, "Any hugs or kisses before we go?"

I turned to Marvin, searching his face for some kind of comfort. But the way he looked at me…

It was as if I was the worst human being on earth.

There was no hug. No kiss. No words of reassurance.

Nothing.

And in that moment, I knew—our marriage would never survive this surgery.

No more kids.

No more passion.

No more us.

A Talk with God

As the tears rolled down my face on the way to the operating room, I had a conversation with God.

"Lord, please give me the strength to get through this."

This wasn't just about me anymore.

I had two children at home who needed their mother. I had to survive—for them.

This battle was personal.

This fight was real.

And with God's help, I would overcome it.

Because through all the pain, all the heartbreak…

Love shall prevail.

4 A STAR IS BORN

As I recovered from my surgery, I found myself trying to figure out what to do next in my complicated life. The procedure had gone well, and I was healing, but I wasn't well enough to take long trips just yet.

That's when my sister, Tywanda, asked if she could take my kids along with her and her children to our annual family reunion on my father's side. Family was something my father took very seriously, and I didn't want my children to miss out on all the fun just because I couldn't go. This year, the reunion was being held in Atlanta, Georgia.

Though I knew my kids, Kori and Alyssa, would have an amazing time, I was nervous. This would be our first time apart since they were born. They were, without a doubt, the loves of my life—my entire world. The thought of separating from them was heartbreaking. I had already made the difficult decision to separate from my cheating husband of seven years, and that was painful enough. But now, my children being gone too? It left me feeling incredibly lonely.

Still, I reminded myself that I needed this break. I needed time to gather my thoughts and process the mess that was my failing marriage.

Letting Go for the First Time

The day before the trip, my children packed their bags with excitement. I made sure they had plenty of snacks and drinks for the long car ride. Knowing my kids, I didn't want them complaining about being starving on the trip. A packed car full of family members meant there was no excuse for them to pretend they were neglected!

As I watched them prepare for their little adventure, I silently prayed that this trip would be a better experience than Libertyland®. No stress. No chaos. Just a simple, fun getaway for my children.

For two days, they would explore, see new things, and make memories with our extended family. That thought alone excited me.

The Big Talent Show

Later, I called them to check in.

They were thrilled.

Excitedly, they tried to tell me everything about their trip. But I asked them to save all the details for when they got home—I wanted to hear it all in person!

A few hours later, they returned home, ecstatic to see their mommy. Tywanda wasted no time telling me about the highlight of the reunion—the family talent show! She explained how Kori, my quiet and shy son, shocked everyone by singing a song at the event. But then she told me what song he had performed.

"Twelve Play."

I froze.

Of all the songs in the world... why would my young son choose to sing that at a family-oriented event?!

Then it hit me.

I loved music. I played albums constantly in my apartment, blasting them on my surround sound stereo. That's exactly where he had heard it.

Still, I couldn't help but wonder... How did he even know the entire song?!

Discovering My Son's Hidden Talent

Tywanda laughed as she told me how Kori had won over the entire family with his performance. At first, I felt a little embarrassed, but then I realized something more important—my son had talent. The inappropriateness of the song quickly faded from my mind. Instead, I marveled at the fact that my little boy had the courage to get on stage and sing in front of a crowd. That was huge.

I started to wonder... what other hidden talents did my children have?

With all the drama in my life—the stress of my failing marriage, my surgery, my emotional struggles—I hadn't even noticed how quickly my kids were growing up. They were becoming their own little individuals.

A Star Was Born

That weekend in Atlanta, my family got to witness something special. A star was born. Kori had always been shy. He kept to himself. He had friends at school and played with kids at home, but he never stood out in a way that made me think he was a performer.

Yet, at that family reunion, he shined. And as his mother, I was beyond proud. I made sure to tell him just how much his performance impressed me, and how deeply proud I was to call him my son.

5 THE BAPTISM

At this particular season in my life, I was still separated from my soon-to-be ex-husband. Marvin would pick up our daughter, Alyssa, every other weekend, and my dear, loving father—who had been there for my son, Kori, from day one—came to get him every single weekend.

Kori spent most of his time at my mother's house after school, seeing her regularly. During the summers, he would also spend time with Mrs. Etta, a beautiful soul who loved me and my children dearly.

My father had changed his life. The things he used to do, he no longer did. He had become a born-again Christian and was devoted to his faith. He attended church every Sunday, participated in Wednesday night Bible study, sang in the choir, and eventually became a deacon.

Through all my struggles, my father, my biological mother, and other supportive women in my life were there for me. I appreciated everything they did for me and my children. My dad had even been the one to walk me down the aisle when I got married years ago.

He knew I was going through some tough times, facing life-changing decisions that didn't just affect me, but my children as well. But in the midst of my pain, I thanked God for my mother and father—for being there when I needed family the most.

Better late than never, I thought.

Sometimes, people don't need you when they're up—but when they're down, that's when your presence is essential.

A Miraculous Revival

It was revival time at New Hope M.B. Church, where my father served as deacon. And in his house, there was no debate—if you were under his roof, you were going to church.

I, however, didn't attend as often as I should.

I took my children every once in a while, but I always had an excuse. I was going through so much in my personal life. Little did I know, that's when you need God the most. I had been baptized as a child and believed in God, but church wasn't high on my list of priorities.

Then something miraculous happened.

Kori had gone to revival service with my father, and that night, something moved in his spirit.

Later, my dad excitedly told me that my eight-year-old son had gone to the altar in tears.

"He wanted to be saved!"

He had received the power of the Holy Ghost.

I was shocked.

I was surprised.

I couldn't believe my baby boy had accepted Jesus Christ as his personal Savior—and I wasn't there to experience this beautiful moment with him.

Shame washed over me.

I should have been right beside him.

A Life-Changing Moment

The following Sunday, Kori was scheduled to be baptized. I made sure I was there to support my baby as he took this powerful step of faith. The preacher and the deacon stood with him. And as they baptized my child in the name of the Father, the Son, and the Holy Ghost, tears streamed down my face.

This was a life-changing moment—not just for him, but for me as well. As soon as Kori emerged from the water, I rushed to grab and hug him.

I was so proud.

But I also knew that as his mother, I had a responsibility.

It was my duty to raise him in the ways of the Lord—to take him to Sunday school, Bible study, and church every Sunday. He needed to learn God's word and understand what baptism truly represented.

This baptism opened my eyes. It showed me how important it was to raise my children to know Christ, to teach them to live for God, so that when the end times came, they would have eternal life in heaven.

A New Commitment

At that moment, I made up my mind. From that day forward, I would raise my children in the church. I would teach them how to pray, how to fast, and how to seek God every single day. Because when they grew older, I wanted them to remember their upbringing, to never depart from their faith, and to be strong children of God.

This was a humbling, joyful experience.

Nothing else in my life mattered more than this moment.

I had a job to do. And with God's help, I was going to make sure my family remained in prayer—every single day.

Because through it all…

God is good.

And in the end…

Love prevails.

6 FREE AT LAST

I had filed for divorce at the beginning of the year. At this point, we had already been separated for months. The family dynamic was no longer there. I remember being at work one day, taking a break, when I decided to call a highly recommended divorce lawyer I had heard about through mutual friends.

Their office was nearby, in the same city as my workplace, so I wouldn't have to travel far. That same evening, after work, I went in for a free consultation to discuss my case. The legal assistant set me up with an appointment for the following week, and during that time, I gathered as much information as I could about the legal process of divorce.

There was one big problem—I had no money to fund my divorce.

But I was willing to do whatever it took.

I would save up. I would ask for a loan—from family, friends, anyone. At this point, I was determined. This was not an easy decision. It was a choice I wouldn't wish on any woman with children.

My kids deserved a household where their mother and father could love them together—where they could grow up in a stable, affectionate home. But that wasn't my reality.

A Hard Pill to Swallow

I had tried everything to save my marriage.

Counseling? Didn't work.

Losing weight? Didn't make a difference.

Praying to be a better wife? Still, nothing changed.

I was out of options.

And the separation only made things harder.

Separation can be a turning point—it can either push people further apart or make them realize what they've lost. For me, it showed me what was already broken.

The Day of the Appointment

When my appointment finally came, I was nervous. This was a life-changing decision, and even though I had plenty of time to think it through, I still found myself asking,

"Am I doing the right thing?"

The lawyer and I discussed all the legal aspects of the divorce, and the next step was clear—I had to inform Marvin that I had officially filed for divorce.

His reaction?

Indifferent.

He wasn't devastated or sorrowful.

By this point, we had already been living separate lives. He had even started a new relationship with someone else. I was certain he was just as ready as I was to move on. The process required a 60-day waiting period—time to reconsider our decision before moving forward. But honestly, there was nothing to reconsider.

We were both ready to move on and get back to our individual lives. I had two children to raise, and Marvin, I assumed, had his own plans. One thing was certain—we were committed to co-parenting for the sake of our kids. They were, and always would be, the most important people in our lives.

April 4, 2003 – The End of an Era

On April 4, 2003, my seven-year marriage officially ended. Two days would be forever etched into my memory: The day I got married. The day I got divorced. I was now officially a single Black mother.

This was never the life I had envisioned for myself.

But life has a way of throwing curveballs—and when it does, you have to swing anyway. Even if you miss, you keep pushing forward.

Finally, It Was Over.

I was free.

Free at last.

Love hurts… but in the end, it will prevail.

7 BACK TO SCHOOL

At this point in my life, I cried every single night before going to bed. As a single parent, I had to seriously think about my future—how I was going to financially provide for my children. During my marriage, Marvin had been the breadwinner. Yes, I worked, but I was mostly a wife and mother, focused on taking care of our home and meeting the needs of our children.

But now?

Now, I was divorced.

Now, I couldn't just work—I needed a steady career.

Working in a factory was no longer part of my plan. I was a single woman now, and I knew in my heart and soul that I had to go back to school.

Unfinished Business

I had started my education years ago, right after high school. But I dropped out when I got my first apartment. I was a teen mom, and at the time, my top priority was providing a home for my three-year-old son. It was the right choice for that season of my life. But now, things were different.

I had a stable home that I was buying.

I had a car that was paid off.

I had no excuse not to go back to school.

I wanted more for myself. I wanted to be more for my children.

A Dream Rekindled

I had always dreamed of becoming a school teacher.

But when I was married, my ex-husband had made it clear:

"We can't afford for you to go back to school. We both need to work to provide for this family."

At the time, I understood. He was the head of the household, and I followed his lead.

My education wasn't a priority for him—probably because he had never gone to college himself.

But now?

Now, it was my choice.

Now, it was my time.

For once, I was putting myself first.

Enrolling at Mississippi State University

I made up my mind—I was going back to college. There was only one university I wanted to attend: Mississippi State University. I had no interest in applying anywhere else. MSU was the best choice for my teaching degree, and I was determined to enroll. That summer, I took the first step and applied. But there was a problem. I didn't have all my financial aid paperwork in order. Panic set in.

I started crying, overwhelmed by the thought that my dream was slipping away.

"What if this doesn't happen?"

"What if I'm not smart enough to go back?"

I had been out of school for so long that I doubted myself. I prayed and asked God for another chance—for the strength to finish the race if He allowed me to start it. Because the truth was, I didn't have enough faith in myself. But then, after two weeks of waiting—

The Letter That Changed Everything

I received my acceptance letter from Mississippi State University. I held it in my hands, barely believing it was real. I rushed to show my children, and together, we celebrated. Their mom had the courage to go back to school.

A Delayed Destiny, Not a Denied One. My journey had been delayed, but it was not denied. Just because I was a divorced, single Black woman didn't mean my life was over. It was just beginning. Things were finally coming together for me and my family. And no matter what happened next…

Love would continue to prevail.

8 LOVE THY NEIGHBOR

It was really happening. I was ecstatic that I was finally furthering my education. As a newly single Black mother, I knew it was imperative that I be able to provide for my children on my own. Everything was slowly falling into place—just as it should. But there was one problem. I didn't have anyone to watch my kids while I was away at school for hours at a time.

A Mother's Concern

The biggest worry on my mind was my children's safety and security while I was away. Since I had to work during the day, my first-semester classes were scheduled at night. I could only work part-time, but I had to maintain a full-time class schedule in order to graduate in two and a half years. At this time, my kids were still young, and the thought of leaving them home alone terrified me.

I started to doubt everything.

Could I really do this?

Finding Help

I didn't want to ask my parents or siblings to babysit. I felt like this was my burden to bear, and I was determined to handle it on my own. But then, I thought of someone special. A kind-hearted woman who had always been a light in my life.

A Special Neighbor

She was my neighbor from across the street. Her two boys and my son were best friends—inseparable. She had only been in the neighborhood a few years, but she had already become known as an amazing babysitter. Her house was always full of kids, and I had observed firsthand how loving, compassionate, and caring she was. She not only took care of her own children, but she also helped so many others. I admired how she provided for them, how she interacted with them, and how she created a safe, welcoming home for so many.

Our boys went to school together, played sports, and spent countless hours playing video games at our house. And my daughter, Alyssa? She adored Jenny. She hugged her every time she saw her, like she was a second mother. I trusted Jenny. And I knew, without a doubt, that she was the one who could help me through this next season of my life.

An Answered Prayer

That weekend, I walked over to Jenny's house and asked if she would be willing to watch my children while I was in school. It was no secret that I was recently single. Everyone in the neighborhood knew that I was now divorced. Jenny looked at me with the warmest smile and said something I will never forget:

"I am so proud of you. And I will not charge you one red cent to watch your kids."

I was speechless.

She told me she admired me for trying to better myself and pursuing my dreams. She saw my struggle, but instead of pity, she encouraged me. She lifted me up on the days I felt too tired from the long drive to and from school. She reminded me why I was doing this—for my children. She told me, over and over again, how proud she was that I had the courage to do what so many other young women wouldn't.

I needed that kind of encouragement in my life. I needed someone who believed in me when I didn't always believe in myself. And God knew exactly who to place in my life.

More Than a Neighbor

I appreciated Jenny more than words could express. She was there for me at a time when I didn't know where to turn. She was more than my neighbor—

She was my friend.

She was my answered prayer.

And I thank God for sending her to me.

Love you, Jenny.

9 DRESS NOT IMPRESS

While waiting for my second semester of classes to begin, I wanted to do something fun with my kids and stay involved in their school activities.

One day, while checking Alyssa's backpack, I came across a flyer for an upcoming school pageant that would be held in the gymnasium during Christmas break. I saw this as the perfect opportunity to create some "dress to impress" memories with my children. I had two beautiful kids, and this was a great chance for the world to see how amazing they were. So, without hesitation, I entered both of them into their school pageant.

The best part? It was a casual wear competition, which meant I didn't have to spend a fortune on renting a tuxedo or a long, flowing gown.

Convincing Alyssa

Kori had no issues with entering the contest. But Alyssa? She had plenty to say. See, my unpredictable child was more interested in wrestling than wearing fancy dresses. Yes, wrestling. I never understood why, but she was obsessed. She knew all the WWE characters, their moves, and their rivalries. She had zero desire to walk across a stage in a dress, smiling and posing.

While I envisioned elegance and pageantry, she preferred to sit in front of the TV watching Monday Night Raw. I knew convincing her to participate in the pageant would not be easy.

Bribery and Negotiations

I considered bribing her. She loved John Cena, and I knew a new action figure of him would get her attention. So, I did what I had to do—because I had already paid the entry fees, and there was no way they were backing out now!

I sat Alyssa down and negotiated a deal. If she participated in the pageant, she could stay up late and watch wrestling—after finishing all her homework, of course.

She agreed.

And just like that, we were off to find her a dress.

The Big Event

We found a simple yet stylish white dress with a scarf, and she was satisfied. Now, all that was left was practice. The kids had to rehearse their routines on the gymnasium stage before the event. All Alyssa had to do was follow the guidelines—walk to the marked tape, smile, and look at the judges. But my kids had never done anything like this before, and I quickly realized that following directions was going to be a challenge. Still, I was in it to win it! I wanted to see my children succeed in something that required nothing but concentration, confidence, and a beautiful smile.

Kori Shines, Alyssa Struggles

Kori competed in the 5th-grade division, and he did an amazing job. He won Most Handsome!

I wasn't shocked at all—I already knew my son was a handsome, dapper young man.

Alyssa, on the other hand, competed in the 1st and 2nd-grade division. She knew our agreement before we left the house. But as she stood on stage, I began to get nervous. She refused to smile. She wouldn't even look at me or the audience. She walked across that stage completely uninterested, ignoring the fact that she was supposed to poise herself, make eye contact with the judges, and show confidence.

When it was over, I praised her, telling her she did a magnificent job. But deep down? I was disappointed.

A Hard Lesson Learned

This pageant meant the world to me. Why? Because I had always wanted to be in a pageant, but never got the chance. I had dreamed of dressing up, putting on beautiful clothing, and stepping onto a stage with grace and confidence. But Alyssa?

She had zero interest in any of it. She participated only because she wanted to watch wrestling—not because she wanted to be there. And that's when I learned a valuable lesson. Never force your children to do something their heart isn't in. After that experience, I never asked Alyssa to enter another pageant. I realized that if she wasn't happy, she wouldn't be her best. And forcing her would only waste both our time.

A Lesson for Every Parent

Let your children be who they are. Not who you want them to be. And as much as I wanted my daughter to love the pageant world, she would rather be watching John Cena throw someone to the mat. And that's okay. Because in the end, her happiness was what truly mattered.

10 YOU ARE THE FATHER

I had just made it home after working a 12-hour shift when my child's father, Charlie, called me.

"I need to speak with you privately," he said.

His voice was urgent—filled with concern and hesitation.

I had never heard him sound this nervous before.

Immediately, I jumped up, put my shoes on, and drove to meet him at the local grocery store uptown. I had no idea what he was about to tell me. But I wasn't prepared for what came next.

An Unexpected Request

See, Charlie was my first love. I had fallen for him as a young teenager—at just 15 years old. He had always been a special person in my life, so I couldn't imagine what could possibly be wrong. Then, he looked me straight in the eyes and said,

"I want a DNA test."

I froze.

"What? A DNA test? After all these years?"

Charlie was questioning Kori's paternity.

I was shocked.

For years, he had been close to his son, spending quality time with him and his family. I had never doubted that Charlie was his father. So, I told him, without hesitation,

"Fine. I have no problem with it."

I wasn't bothered by the process of testing my son.

But Kori was confused.

"Why do I have to do this?" he asked.

I had to explain to him that this was important to his father, and at this point, we needed to go through with it for his sake.

Taking the Test

Two weeks later, we had an appointment at the testing center. Charlie arrived before us, clearly eager to get answers. I walked in confident that this would soon be over and would prove him wrong. After the test, we went about our lives, waiting for the results to arrive in the mail.

Then, two weeks later, Charlie called me first. His voice was devastated.

"Kori is not my son."

A Painful Truth

I stood there in shock.

"No. That has to be a mistake!" I said.

I refused to believe it.

I even wondered if they had given us the wrong results.

But deep down, I knew.

It was true.

After all these years, I had made a horrible mistake.

I had cheated on Charlie out of revenge, and another man—Devin—was Kori's father. I begged Charlie for forgiveness, but he didn't want to hear it. I had been so in love with him as a young, immature teen, and in my foolishness, I had believed that the man you had the most intimate moments with would surely be the father of your child.

I was wrong.

And now, I had embarrassed not just myself, but my son.

Finding the Truth

Despite the shame, I knew I had to do the right thing. Kori deserved to know the truth. He needed to know his real father, his real family, and his true bloodline.

After some time, I reached out to Devin. I explained everything and asked him to take a DNA test. I knew this would be a hard pill to swallow, but I also knew that I couldn't let fear or embarrassment stop me from getting the truth for my child. At first, Kori didn't want to go through the process again. I understood. But I helped him see that this was important—for his sake.

I prayed. I asked God for strength and guidance, because I

couldn't do this alone.

The Final Test

Finally, Devin agreed to take the test. I scheduled a private appointment, making sure we kept it between us until we knew the results. We took the test. And then, we waited again. Two weeks later, Devin got his results first—just like Charlie had.

Then, he called me.

"He is my son. 99.99%."

I burst into tears. Not out of pain—but out of relief.

Cleaning Up My Mistakes

For too long, I had been living in the chaos of uncertainty—believing one thing, only to find out the truth was something else entirely. This was something I had to clean up from my teenage years, and now, as a grown woman and a single mother, I had no choice but to face it head-on.

I knew there would be whispers and judgment. Embarrassment followed me everywhere. But I didn't care. All that mattered was that my son knew his father.

A Hard Lesson Learned

There was nothing in this world I wouldn't do to hear his real father say: "I am his father."

I would go to the ends of the earth for my children. No matter the cost. No matter the pain. Because through it all, I learned one undeniable truth— "Mama's baby, Papa's maybe" is real. And still…

Love will prevail.

11 CLASS OF '08

The years were flying by, and my children and I were thriving tremendously. They were growing up so fast, achieving great things, and making me prouder by the day. Kori was involved in sports—football, basketball, and track—while Alyssa was busy with basketball and cheerleading as her hobbies. As for me?

I was working two jobs while trying to finish college, a journey I had started years earlier. Since I could only take a few classes at a time, I had to be patient. But patience was something I didn't have much of at this stage in my life. I needed my degree so I could fully provide for my children. I had no choice but to push forward, and I refused to make excuses about why I couldn't succeed.

The Struggle to Succeed

I never liked the idea of receiving government assistance like food stamps or housing aid. Yes, I had used programs like Lift, INC to help pay for my utilities and mortgage, but to me, it felt like a handout. And I was too proud to continue relying on it. My mother called me stubborn, saying I always wanted to do everything on my own. She wasn't wrong.

But even though I wanted to be independent, I was still grateful for the support that helped me stay afloat while completing my education.

A Double Graduation – A Moment to Remember

The year was 2008, and it was finally happening—

Kori was about to graduate from high school… and so was I! We were both graduating in the same month—May. What an incredible moment this was! When I was getting fitted for my cap and gown, so was he. When I had graduation practice, so did he.

It was an amazing feeling to share this once-in-a-lifetime experience with my son—walking across our respective stages to receive something we had worked so hard for.

2008 was a year we would never forget.

Overcoming the Past

Kori and I had been through so much together—

The DNA test.

The heartache.

The trauma.

Yet, he never let any of it hold him back from getting his education. Kori was a brilliant, well-mannered young man. His teachers had nothing but praise for him throughout his school years. They thought the world of him—and so did I. I knew in my heart that he could be anything he wanted to be in life, as long as he stayed humble and continued to trust in God. My father had raised us in the church, teaching us to pray and depend on God in everything we did. And now, that faith was paying off.

Graduation Day – A Proud Mother's Moment

Kori's graduation ceremony was held outside on the football field. Vardaman High School did a phenomenal job with the decorations, memorabilia, and the video tributes showcasing sporting events and highlights from the Class of '08.

It was a beautiful night.

His father, Devin, along with my dad, our family, and our friends, all came out to celebrate with us. It was a momentous occasion—one filled with pride, love, and joy. And then came the icing on the cake—

Kori earned a leadership scholarship to the college of his choice, where he would begin in the fall. We were beyond proud of him. As his parents, grandparents, family, and friends, we showered him with so much love that night.

A Well-Deserved Celebration

To his surprise, I had planned a graduation party at the house. A young Black male graduating high school was an accomplishment in itself. Far too many drop out, but Kori didn't.

He persevered.

We were blessed.

That night, the house was full of his friends, celebrating and laughing. I hoped I wouldn't regret letting a group of teenagers party in my living room—but thankfully, they mostly stayed outside in the yard. Kori was so happy, and that's all that mattered. His friends were still at the house at 2 A.M., but I didn't say a word. As long as they were safe and not out drinking and driving, I was fine with them celebrating as long as they wanted. It was his special day, and we made sure it was one to remember.

My Own Graduation – A Bittersweet Victory

A few days later, it was my turn to receive my college degree. But Kori had a football banquet that same night, and most of my family was unable to attend my ceremony. I was devastated. I had worked so hard for this moment. But I didn't let it break me. I walked across that stage with my head high, receiving my degree with pride.

A Year to Remember

2008 was a year that Kori and I would never forget. The year we both achieved a milestone. The year we both proved to ourselves and to the world that with faith, hard work, and determination—

All things are possible.

12 HE SAVED ME

One Sunday morning, the children and I got up and started getting ready for church service. From the moment we began, it felt like one issue after another. I couldn't find my favorite pair of heels. Alyssa was moving too slowly in the bathroom. Kori hadn't ironed his shirt. I started to wonder if we should have just waited until next Sunday. We were so unorganized and unprepared, but I knew we needed to be there.

A Journey Back to God

God had blessed us tremendously—

We had endured losses.

We had been through surgeries.

We had survived DNA tests and everything else life threw at us.

It hadn't been easy for us to bounce back from our trials and tribulations. So the question was never about whether we would serve the Lord—

It was about remembering why we needed to go. God had to remain the center of our lives if we were going to withstand the attacks of the enemy. And that morning, it seemed as if the enemy was working overtime to distract us from going to church.

Making It to Church

Somehow, we finally got dressed and made it out the door. We had a children's nursery where Alyssa could learn about the Bible, and Kori was old enough to sit in the congregation as an adult. That morning, the pastor preached on John 3:16—

"For God so loved the world, that He gave His only begotten Son, that whosoever believeth in Him should not perish, but have everlasting life."

As I sat there, I felt a mighty rushing wind sweep through my body. Something was stirring in my soul. I had been at church before, but I had never been in the church. I had believed in God, but I had never truly experienced the power of the Holy Ghost.

But that day?

Everything changed.

A Divine Encounter

When it was time for the altar call, the pastor asked, "Is there anyone who would love to give me their hand and God their heart?"

Before I even realized what was happening, I found myself walking to the front. I didn't remember making the decision to move. That's when I knew—

It wasn't me.

It was God, piercing my soul, calling me back to Him.

See, I knew that Jesus loved me, but I had been saying I loved Him without being willing to keep His commandments or live according to His will. But on that very day, I was saved.

It was like nothing I had ever experienced before—

So magical.

So renewing.

So refreshing.

A Changed Woman

Tears streamed down my face as I began to thank God for saving my broken soul. From that moment forward, I committed to living for Him to the best of my ability. I still didn't know what my calling was, but I knew I would seek His will until I found out.

That Sunday, I walked into the church one way, and I walked out completely different.

Spreading the Joy

On Monday morning, I went to work beaming with excitement. I couldn't stop smiling. I told my co-workers how the Lord had saved me, and my heart felt so full of joy, love, and renewal. I never wanted this encounter with God to fade away. I had been transformed. And no matter what happened next, one thing was certain—

God's love will always prevail.

13 MY TRUE PURPOSE

After finishing school, I found myself at a crossroads, trying to figure out where I wanted to be in my career. I felt drawn toward helping others—especially those who couldn't help themselves.

Looking back, I realized that assisting others had been a part of my life for as long as I could remember. But why? Why was I always so passionate about making those in need a priority in my daily life? Then, I thought about my sister. She was one of the first people I ever had the privilege of helping.

A Calling from Childhood

When my sister was a toddler, our family discovered that she was hearing impaired. She was just three years old when we learned she couldn't hear or speak. She needed hearing aids to communicate effectively. I remember feeling an overwhelming desire to make her life easier, not harder. So, as a young girl myself, I took it upon myself to teach her how to read and write. She was an eager student, catching on quickly, and soon, she was able to communicate in a way that made things easier for her—and for our family.

That experience stayed with me.

It shaped me. And it led me to pray about my future.

I asked God to reveal His will for my life—

How could I use my gifts to inspire and uplift others?

A Divine Assignment

Not long after, I applied for a job at a behavioral facility for children. I wasn't sure if I had the skills or patience for the job, but something kept pulling me toward it. I had driven past the facility many times, and each time, my eyes were drawn to that place.

I prayed:

"God, is this where You need me to be?"

I had heard so many dreadful stories about that facility. But I was just one woman—eager to start somewhere, eager to make a difference.

The Opportunity That Changed Everything

Two weeks after my interview, I got the call back. The human resources director invited me to attend orientation. I should have been excited. Instead? I was terrified. Because I understood the assignment all too well. I had once been a struggling teen who needed guidance. Now, it was my turn to be that guide for someone else.

More Than Just a Job

My goal and ambition were clear—

To please God while using my gifts to help others. This was never about money. This was about mentorship. I had two children of my own, and God had blessed me with the ability to nurture them. Now, He was giving me the opportunity to be a blessing to others. I often reminded myself:

"God never gave up on me, so I will never give up on His children."

They were our hope for tomorrow.

They needed guidance, patience, and love from people who truly cared about their well-being.

Paying It Forward

God had given me a gift—and after everything I had endured as a child, I was determined to pay it forward. Children are a blessing from God, and I knew it was my purpose to help them see their own worth. Through patience and love, I watched as children with behavioral struggles grew into model citizens—proof that with the right guidance, anyone could thrive. I couldn't have been prouder to be part of something so meaningful.

Love had prevailed in my life—

Just as I always knew it would.